CURTIS INTERNATIONAL
PORTRAITS OF GREATNESS

•

General Editor
Enzo Orlandi

Text by
Mario Rivoire

Translator
C. J. Richards

Published by
ARNOLDO MONDADORI EDITORE
and
THE CURTIS PUBLISHING COMPANY

THE
LIFE
&
TIMES
OF
NAPOLEON

CP
CURTIS BOOKS
A division of
The Curtis Publishing Company
Philadelphia • New York

FROM CORSICA: THE EAGLE FLIES

Below, two illustrations depicting scenes of Napoleon's childhood. In the first, by Raffet, he is shown with members of his family in the house where he was born. The priest is his maternal uncle, the future Cardinal Fesch, who rose to prominence after his nephew had come to power. The second, a lithograph by Horace Vernet, shows young Bonaparte as a cadet at the Brienne military

school, which he entered on April 25, 1779, and left in 1784, at the age of 15, to enter the Ecole Militaire of Paris. To the right, a contemporary print depicting the last episode of the Corsican period of Napoleon's life: The unsuccessful revolutionary expedition against Sardinia, which at that time, February, 1793, still belonged to the House of Savoy.

On her return from church on Assumption Day (August 15) of the year 1769, so the story goes, Letizia Ramolino, wife to Carlo Bonaparte, gave birth, on a threadbare rug, to their second son, Napoleon. Overcome with labor pains, she had been unable to reach her bed. The story doubtless is apocryphal but in keeping with Napoleon's lifelong hurry to reach his destination (and destiny). Legend adds the equally unlikely detail that in the rug, on which the birth took place, were woven heroic scenes and figures from the *Iliad*. "Madame Mère," as Letizia Bonaparte was later to be known, dismissed the whole story with a laugh and the prosaic admission that their Corsican home contained nothing so luxurious as rugs, and even if it had, by August the rugs would certainly have been taken up. The story is typical of those relating to his early childhood in Ajaccio. Spun out of hearsay, they were of no interest to Napoleon himself, who never harked back to his earliest years.

The Bonapartes were a family in modest circumstances of the lesser nobility. At Napoleon's birth the island had only just passed from the hands of the Genoese to those of the French King (Louis XV). Carlo Bonaparte, a realist, made himself useful to the new rulers. Having become a Representative of the Nobles of Corsica, he managed to obtain for his second son (the first one was destined for the Church) a scholarship to the military school at Brienne, an institution run by a religious order, from which, in 1784 he moved on to the Ecole Militaire in Paris. When he left this on October 28, 1785, he was a 2nd lieutenant in the artillery.

Two years after the outbreak of the French Revolution, on July 6, 1791, at Venice where he was garrisoned, Napoleon took an oath to defend the new regime. He then returned to Corsica to spread the new revolutionary gospel. At first he backed Pasquale Paoli, the apostle of Corsican independence, but later, when he saw possible conflict between Paoli's aims and those of the French, he shifted his loyalty. He had also soon realized that the Corsican cause would be a dead end for him, and so he abandoned it to embrace a cause which offered real scope to his abilities and ambitions.

The only consistency in his actions stems from his own individual view of freedom: maximum personal freedom was to be achieved only by means of maximum personal power.

To the left, an anonymous etching of the capitulation of Toulon in December, 1793. Toulon had fallen into the hands of the English, who had been welcomed with open arms by its inhabitants, most of whom were Royalists. The Republican Army laid siege to it, but this was not brought to a successful close without some disagreement between the civilian observers sent by the Convention (the French Government which lasted from September, 1792, to October, 1795), who wanted a frontal attack, and the army command led by Napoleon, who opposed it. Dual control of the conduct of war is nothing new. By clever use of cannon fire, he demolished one of the forts which closed off the harbor roadstead, thus forcing the English fleet to put to sea. Below, Napoleon shown confined to quarters. July 27, 1794 (9 Thermidor of the Year II in the revolutionary calendar), marked the end of the Reign of Terror. On this day the Jacobin dictatorship was overthrown by a number of deputies of the Convention; Robespierre "the incorruptible" was executed, and another pack of wolves, this time called the Directory, took over. Chief among these was Barras who was later instrumental, though sometimes unwittingly, in bringing Napoleon to power. But the latter's rise was not immediate; in fact, he took a few steps backward at this juncture. As soon as the new government had taken over, he was placed under arrest and temporarily deprived of his rank as brigadier general, a rank to which he had been promoted for his brilliant maneuvering at Toulon. He was soon reinstated but without a command.

A HAPPY MARRIAGE

On October 5, 1795 (13 Vendémiaire of the Year IV) a Parisian mob threatened the Convention. Napoleon, who was available, seemed the logical man to quell the riot. The clash occurred off the Rue St.-Honoré. Below, Napoleon's troops fire on the insurgents from the steps of the Church of St. Roch. On October 26 the Convention went out of existence and the Directory took over to prolonged cheers of "Long live the Republic." Public reaction to the freedom of the press is reflected in the print at the bottom of the page. Joséphine de Beauharnais's portrait, to the right, is an enlargement of a miniature by Isabey, done in 1798.

A man on his way up needs a wife, preferably one who has access to the best social and political circles. Marie-Rose Joséphine Tascher de la Pagerie, widow of General de Beauharnais, mother of his two children, Eugène and Hortense, mistress to Barras, had all the necessary qualifications including the not negligible one of being ravishingly beautiful. After the events of October 5, 1795 (13 Vendémiaire) the Convention had ordered the complete disarmament of Paris. Such rigorous measures to enforce the decree had been taken that even the sword of a dead General of the Republic had been confiscated. That general had been Alexandre de Beauharnais, who was guillotined during the Reign of Terror. His son Eugène went to Napoleon to plead for the return of his father's sword. Bonaparte, unable to resist the boy's appeal, granted his request. Madame de Beauharnais, much moved by the gesture, called on the youthful general to express her thanks. They fell in love—or so the story goes—but whatever the circumstances, Joséphine had no difficulty in making the impressionable young general love her. It is quite likely that the clever widow saw in him a way out of her difficulties. After all her vicissitudes and adventures, she needed the security of marriage. It is also not improbable that if she really did scheme to ensnare him, the prudent counsels of Barras strengthened her inclinations. Consequently, on March 9, 1796, Napoleon and Joséphine were married in Paris, at a civil ceremony. On the marriage certificate Napoleon made himself out to be 18 months older than he was and gave Paris as his birthplace. Joséphine subtracted four years from her age. The ceremony as such, when it finally took place, was decidedly brief. The groom was two hours late; the presiding official, citizen Leclerc, had fallen asleep in a chair. "Wake up, Citizen, and marry us quickly," said the general, shaking him. He was, as always, in a hurry. The honeymoon was brief. Two days later a post chaise drew up to the bride's house in Rue Chantereine into which the groom had moved. Bonaparte climbed into the carriage, waved farewell, and went on his way to the Italian border. He had just been appointed Commander-in-Chief of the French Army in Italy.

His hastily ordered departure set tongues wagging. It was said that Joséphine's lover wanted her husband out of the way. The tone of Napoleon's letters to his faraway bride only add credence to the story, overflowing as they were with passionate protestations of love, outbursts of jealousy and apparently well-justified recriminations.

Bridges and rivers were apparently of prime importance in the Italian campaign. At the bottom of the page, the battle of the Adda River bridge at Lodi on May 10, 1796, by Lejeune. To the right, Gros's famous painting of Napoleon at the bridge of Arcole over the Adige River on November 16–17, 1796. These were two outstanding events in the lightning Napoleonic campaign which had started with the defeat of the Piedmontese and ended with the preliminary peace negotiations with Austria at Leoben. These preliminary terms formed the basis for the Treaty of Campoformio signed in October, 1797. Immediately below, Napoleon at Millesimo, site of an Austrian defeat on April 14, 1796.

ITALY: FIRST VICTORIES

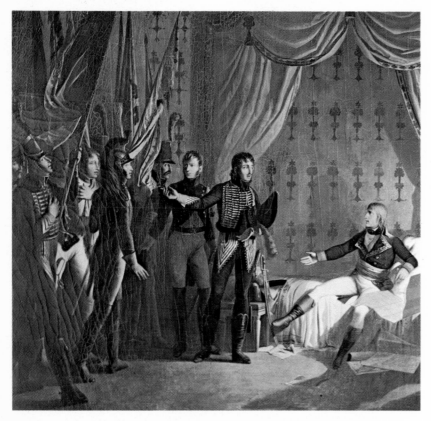

The Italian campaign was to be a three-pronged offensive planned by Lazare Carnot, a former member of the Convention, who had become one of the five members of the Directory. The Army of Italy was to advance upon Vienna, invading the Paduan Plain and marching through the valley of the Adige. The other two armies, one of the Sambre and Meuse under the command of General Jourdan, the other of the Rhine and Moselle under the command of General Moreau, were likewise to march upon the capital of the Hapsburgs. Bonaparte was a past master at making the most of his enemies' mistakes. Although his troops were greatly outnumbered by the Austrians, he engaged in preliminary skirmishes which effectively divided the enemy. He managed in this way always to outnumber the forces he was engaging in battle at the moment and then he defeated them. His plan was simple and direct. He first defeated the Piedmontese at Millesimo on April 14, 1796, and immobilized them by the armistice signed at Cherasco. This had not been authorized by the Directory, but he paid little attention to the directives from his government when they did not suit his plans. On May 15 he entered Milan; between May and June he forced armistices upon the Dukes of Parma and Modena and upon the Holy See. His troops occupied Leghorn. Wherever he went he levied heavy indemnities on the local population and raided museums and palaces for works of art. These were dispatched to Paris to mollify the Directory, a sugar-coating for the bitter pill of his insubordination. Side by side with his military operations he was reorganizing the political setup of the Italian peninsula. He created the Cispadane and Transpadane republics, to which he gave constitutions based on the French one. Under the pretext that the Duke of Modena had secretly helped Austria, he broke the armistice and on October 8, 1796, he annexed the duke's territories to the Transpadane Republic. On October 9 he granted, with decidedly ungenerous conditions, French protection to the Republic of Genoa. The next day he signed a peace treaty with Naples. On November 5 the Grand Duke of Tuscany also obtained peace at a heavy price. There was still little progress shown in the peace negotiations with the Pope because of questions of a spiritual nature raised by the Directory. However, that settlement, though only a provisional one, was not long delayed. Wherever he went, Bonaparte tried to leave order in his wake.

AN ARMY
IN RAGS

Like all the great actors of history, Napoleon created his own legend. His stirring proclamation to the ragged, demoralized, unkempt hordes that made up the Army of Italy whipped them into shape as no previous commander had been able to do: "Soldiers, you are hungry and almost naked... I will lead you into the most fertile plains on earth... There you shall find honor, glory, riches: Soldiers of Italy, can resolution fail you now?" And he set about fashioning what in those days and in comparison with the other armies of the Republic must have seemed the very model of a tightly ordered, well-disciplined army. When Napoleon took over, the quartermaster had run out of money; because of this, supplies of flour from Genoa had been cut off and all provisioning by the commissary's meager distributing force of 150 pack horses and mules had been discontinued, with the exception of olive oil, which was still plentiful. The officials in charge stole right and left and wallowed in ease and luxury in Nice. Napoleon's predecessor as commander of this army had been Schérer, a man in his 60's, a calamity for both the times and the post he occupied. He operated only by the book of rules, never displaying either imagination or initiative. He was fired not one moment too soon. Napoleon negotiated for loans amounting to about 7,000,000 lire which were to buy the support of Italian Revolutionaries for the French. Napoleon's scheme was not to attack the native population but to negotiate with them secretly to pay for the fruits of victory (a forerunner of the fifth column perhaps?).

Through a succession of proclamations, resounding like fanfares, the new commander aroused the fighting ardor of his men. His legend was now well launched, embellished by his enemies' darkling descriptions of a villainous pack of pitiless brigands ready for any depredation or violence. And his foes found comfort in laying the blame for their own lack of success in opposing him on his unorthodox methods. How could they win against an antagonist who did not play according to the rules of the game? The army Napoleon had found upon his arrival in Italy had been made up of disorganized bands of unpaid raggedly dressed men, soldiers of the Republic; what he left was a tightly knit army consisting of well-paid smartly uniformed soldiers who were already calling themselves Soldiers of Napoleon, the forerunners of the "*Grande Armée*."

Bonaparte at Rivoli by Philippoteaux.
This battle, fought on
broken ground near the
Adige River in Northern Italy,
was one of the decisive battles
of the Italian campaign. The
Commander-in-Chief was himself
twice surrounded by the
enemy and had more than one
horse killed under him.

THE AUSTRIAN DEFEAT

The defenders of Mantua leave the city and file out unarmed in front of the victors' banners. The humiliation of General Wurmser and of his men on February 3, 1797, is the subject of the painting by Lecomte, below. Very soon after this the news of the preliminary peace negotiations of Leoben gave rise to great public celebrations in France and to public mourning in Austria. Debucourt's print, below, depicts street vendors engaged in the thriving business of selling pictures of the victorious general. His great asset was that he brought temporary peace. Hereafter his steadily rising popularity could no longer be ignored by the politicians.

It is all too easy, looking down the span of years, to see the Italian campaign as a series of uninterrupted victories which left the enemy breathless. The reality was quite different. On the evening of the victory of Arcole, November 17, 1796, after three days of battle, Louis Bonaparte, Napoleon's brother and aide-de-camp, wrote gloomily to a friend: "The troops have changed; they are asking for peace." Four days before, the General had warned Paris: "We may well be on the verge of losing Italy." But by miraculous efforts he succeeded in rebuilding the morale of his men. He won the battles of Rivoli on January 14, 1797, and of Tagliamento on March 16, 1797. In a lightning maneuver he overtook the armies of his fellow generals and thrust the vanguards into Semmering, 54 miles from Vienna. The Austrians asked for a truce on April 7; on the 18th, at Leoben, the preliminary peace treaty was signed. Bonaparte had won the war. He had done more: he had dictated his own conditions, not the Directory's, for peace. The treaty in its final form was ratified at Campo Formio on October 18. On December 5, 1797, Napoleon Bonaparte was given a triumphal reception in Paris.

THE LURE OF
THE NEAR EAST

During the dark days after Toulon, Bonaparte, who was unoccupied, had asked to be sent to Turkey to organize the Sultan's artillery. After the victories in Italy, he again considered the Near East. He suggested to the approving Directory the conquest of Egypt. His purpose was to interfere with British access to India. He set sail in May of 1798, took Malta, landed in Egypt at the end of June, and reached the Pyramids. But Nelson's victory at the Battle of the Nile in August of 1798, at which the French fleet was sunk, sealed the fate of this particular enterprise. The Sultan of Turkey then took steps to reconquer Egypt, of which he was titular head. After an expedition to Syria, where the plague had decimated the French troops, and after a Pyrrhic land victory at Aboukir against the Turks, Bonaparte put an end to what he called "a romantic interlude." Disquieting news from the home political front persuaded him to leave Egypt, which he did in secret. Slipping through the English naval blockade, he landed in Fréjus, on the French Mediterranean coast, on October 9, 1799, thereby dealing a staggering blow to the French politicians who had hoped to keep him at a distance.

If only because of its exotic aura, the Egyptian and Syrian campaign is one Napoleonic enterprise which best lent itself to pictorial glorification. The paintings to the right and below are only two among the many which recall the campaign. The one opposite, by Gros, who was dubbed the Homer of the Napoleonic Epic, shows a high point in the battle of the Pyramids, which took place on July 21, 1798. Just before this battle, at which the Bey of Cairo was defeated, Napoleon, pointing to the Pyramids, addressed to his troops the famous words: "Soldiers, forty centuries look down upon you." Napoleon is here surrounded by some of his

most famous companions at arms. The painting below, by Lejeune, is a detail of the French victory at the land battle of Aboukir on July 15, 1799. However, despite the profusion of paintings, this particular period in Napoleon's career was little more than a parenthesis. When Bonaparte quit Egypt, he left his expeditionary force in the care of General Kléber, an able and realistic commander who was assassinated within two years. Menou, his successor, was obliged to capitulate in August, 1801, to a British Expeditionary Force which repatriated the surviving 30,000 French forces in Egypt—about half of their original strength.

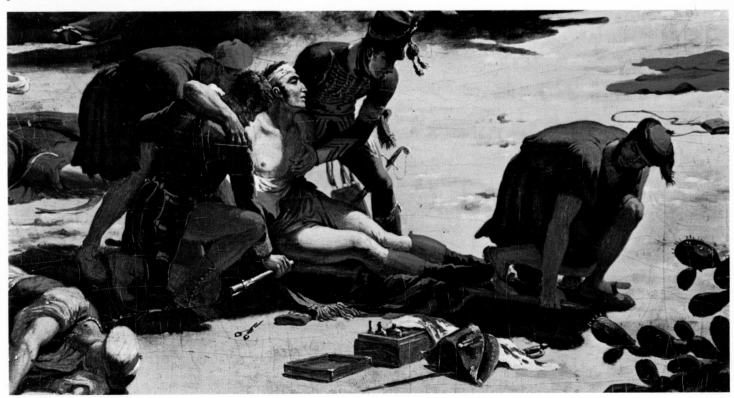

THE GRENADIERS: GUARDIANS OF THE CONSULATE

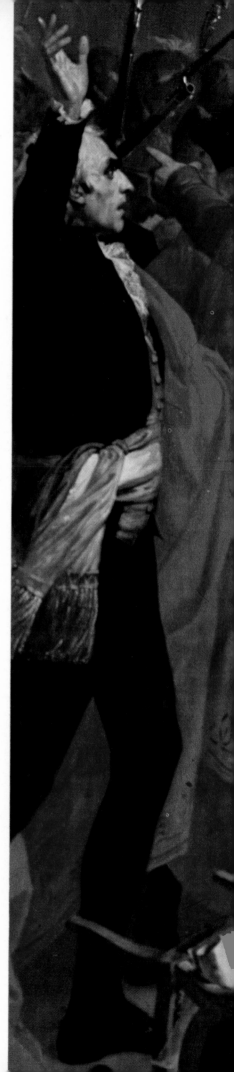

"What has happened to our glorious France? What have you done to her? I gave you victories; I find defeats. I brought you riches from Italy; I find crippling taxes and destitution! What has happened to the thousands of Frenchmen who were my friends, who shared my glory? They are dead!" Napoleon, in this outburst to Barras upon his return from Egypt, was echoing the sentiment of the people. If ever a country was ripe for dictatorship, that country was France. But the choice of a dictator had yet to be made.

In order to foil an alleged Jacobin plot the transfer to Saint-Cloud of the legislative chambers had been ordered. (These two chambers, the Council of Elders and the Council of Five Hundred, had been set up by the Constitution of 1795.) General Bonaparte, the commander of the troops in the Paris region, was put in charge of the operation that was to be carried out on the morning of November 9, 1799. This is known as the famous coup of the 18 Brumaire. All went smoothly in the Council of Elders, but on the following day the Council of Five Hundred balked. Napoleon was greeted, as he entered the chamber, by threatening growls of "Outlaw!" His brother Lucien, president of the Council, correctly sizing up the situation at a glance, rushed out, then returned with the Grenadier Guards. The Deputies were routed and the coup finished. The French Revolutionary Republic had, in fact, ceased to exist.

Opposite, Bouchot's famous painting entitled Le 18 Brumaire. The Grenadiers, led by General Leclerc rush forward to protect Bonaparte, who is surrounded by hostile Deputies. Some of these fled through the window, leaving in their wake rich cloaks and plumed hats which were later appropriated by the Grenadiers. Above, a contemporary print of one of the many cafés where political figures met. These cafés were a natural development of the regional headquarters that had existed briefly in Paris toward the end of the 18th century where animated discussions of a political nature took place. Skepticism and discontent had soon replaced the fiery revolutionary spirit, and admiration for the government had given way to contempt for its officials. The five members of the Directory had been rechristened "the five monkeys."

THE FIRST
AND ONLY CONSUL

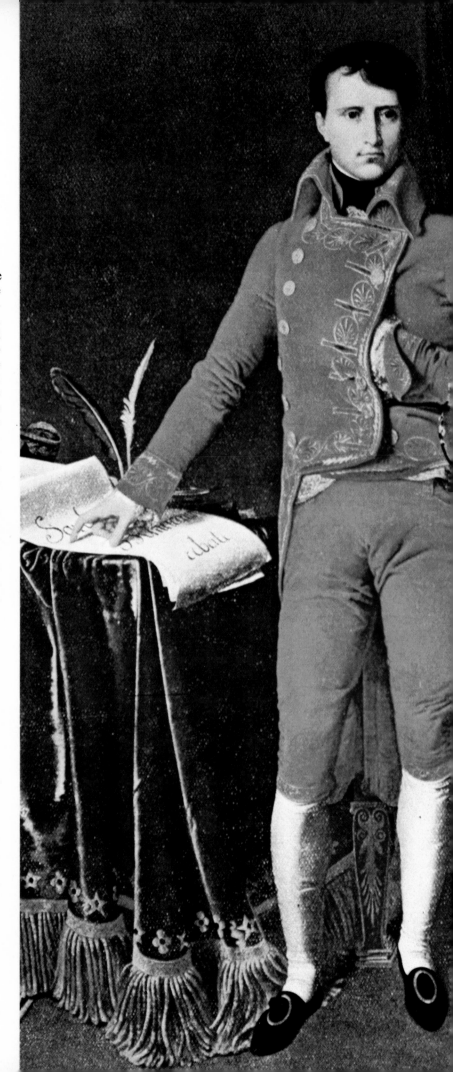

The coup d'état of the 18 Brumaire was validated by the Constitution of December 13, 1799 (22 Frimaire of the year VIII). The France of the Revolution had consumed a great number of constitutions. The first one, in 1791, had marked the still-birth of the constitutional monarchy; the second one, in 1793, had never set up anything at all; the third one, in 1795, had created the Directory. In actual fact, all these constitutions had remained mere documents which put forth declarations of principles that bore little relation to reality. The fourth one was, in this respect, no different from the others. It was solemnly ratified, as the others had been, by a plebiscite; it entrusted the executive power to three consuls appointed for a term of 10 years and eligible for re-election. But the power was really vested in the hands of the First Consul, Napoleon Bonaparte, who took up residence in the palace of the Tuileries on February 19, 1800 (30 Pluviôse of the year VIII).

There was a number of surprises in store for his colleagues: he seemed to know everything that went on; he was unexpectedly hard-working, conscientious and thorough; he expected his subordinates to display equal zeal. As so often happens when a dictatorship is set up, the first reforms instituted were desperately needed and seemed providential to a war-weary and disillusioned public. (This was why the Romans, centuries ago, had prudently limited to a very short duration what they considered an emergency form of government.)

He laid down the principles of a unifying code, which the French had lacked until then, which gave a single set of laws to the entire country. He set up the Council of State, the supreme legislative, judiciary and administrative organ of the government. He revised the tax laws, revalued the currency, reorganized everything in and out of sight; in short, laid down the foundations of modern administration and paved the way, with his legal reforms, for the Napoleonic Code, which has survived almost intact to this day. He pacified the Vendée, a region in the northwest of France, which had remained staunchly royalist and Catholic; he began the peace negotiations with the Church which became the Concordat of August 15, 1801; he granted a number of political amnesties. On August 2, 1802, the Senate, another body set up by the Consulate, having ratified the Peace of Amiens with England on May 25, 1802, proclaimed Napoleon Bonaparte Consul for life. The dictatorship was now permanently established.

Pope Pius VII (Barnaby Chiaramonti), elected to the Holy See in March, 1800, signed the Concordat with France in 1801 after long-drawn-out negotiations. Below, left, in Wicar's drawing, Cardinal Consalvi, his Secretary of State, presents the document to him. There is a wealth of minute detail in Couder's painting, below right, of the setting up, on December 25, 1799, of the Council of State at the Luxembourg Palace. With Napoleon are shown the other two Consuls, Cambacérès and Lebrun. Civilian dress, complete with knee breeches, had become more prevalent than military uniforms. The revolutionary "sans-culottes" had hated and banned this fashion favored by the aristocracy of the Old Regime. The First Consul's various residences became the gathering places of the new society. Among them was La Malmaison, shown at the bottom of the page in Viger's painting. The Temple of Love is in the background. At the far left, Ingres's portrait of Napoleon as First Consul.

Below, two contemporary prints showing French setbacks. Directly below, the assassination, on April 28, 1799 (9 Floréal of the year VII) of three French plenipotentiaries who had been invited to Rastadt, in the Grand Duchy of Bavaria, to negotiate with representatives from Vienna. Meantime the Austrian forces were gaining ground against the French, who were rapidly losing Italy. The intervention of Russia with 80,000 men seriously jeopardized French supremacy in the peninsula. General Suvorov defeated the French in two quick successive battles, one at Cassano on the Trebbia River and the other at Novi. Things were going better for the French on other fronts. The second print shows a detail from one of these battles. Opposite, Thévenin's painting of Napoleon's forces crossing the Alps. On the overleaf, Lejeune's painting shows some of the chief actors in the battle of Marengo: Napoleon in the lower left; Desaix center left, falling from his horse.

MARENGO: THE EVE OF THE EMPIRE

On Christmas Day, 1799, Napoleon had personally written letters to the Emperor of Austria and to the King of England proposing peace; these were not well received. In the spring military operations were resumed. The French Army of the Rhine, under the command of Moreau, defeated the Austrians in early May, pushing them back to the Danube and beyond. It was now Napoleon's turn. On May 6, 1800, he left Paris, retraced Hannibal's footsteps and with a speed that left a deep impression on the popular imagination crossed the Great Saint Bernard Pass between May 15 and 20. On June 2, less than a month later, Napoleon arrived in Milan. His plan had now developed in all its blinding clarity: fill the gap left by the Austrians between their German and Italian forces, deflect the enemy's major strength and make a massive attack.

On the military plane the situation was such that one battle could decide the outcome of the war. There was such a battle: Marengo, on June 14.

The great battle which took place near Alessandria actually consisted of two separate battles. It began at 6 A.M. Bonaparte advanced on the plain with his troops disposed in fan-shaped columns. The Austrian forces, led by General Melas, suddenly sprang upon them. For four hours two columns of French troops withstood the onslaught of the Austrians, who had just forded the Bormida, a nearby stream, but they finally had to retreat. The reserves called in by Napoleon likewise fell back and more ground was lost. By 3 P.M. the Austrian commander had defeated the French and gone to rest at nearby Alessandria. At 5 P.M. Desaix and his corps appeared on the battlefield, offered to lead another attack and by sunset had routed the Austrians, who fell back in total disorder across the Bormida. From the battlefield Napoleon wrote to the Emperor in Vienna. His tone was no longer that of a general, but that of a head of state to an equal. He proffered peace; the rest was up to the Emperor.

A MUSHROOMING OF REPUBLICS

There was a great outburst of joy when news of the victory of Marengo reached the French capital. Cambacérès, one of the three consuls, remarked that for the first time in nine years there took place "a truly spontaneous public celebration." Marengo was a victory, but above all, it was a promise of peace.

But peace was not yet to be had. The negotiations started at Lunéville on November 5, 1800, were proceeding very slowly. On November 22, hostilities were resumed. Some 10 days later, General Moreau, of the Army of the Rhine fame, spearheading his forces on the Inn River, met the Austrians on terrain of his own choosing and defeated them soundly at the battle of Hohenlinden on December 3, 1800. This was the first major French victory won by someone other than Napoleon.

Moreau followed the defeated remnants down to Vienna. On Christmas Day, the Austrians, determined to save their capital, asked for an armistice. The peace treaty was finally signed at Lunéville on February 9, 1801, by representatives of the Austrian emperor and of the French Government. The King of Naples, ally of the English and of the Austrians, added his signature to the peace treaty on March 29. Paul I, Tsar of Russia, who had once sent an expeditionary force to Italy, had already retired from the struggle. The coalition engineered in 1798 by the English was at an end.

One year later, on March 25, 1802, England also signed a peace treaty, at Amiens. France had finally realized her age-long dream of stretching her boundaries to the Rhine. In the orbit of her Republic there was now a constellation of sister (or daughter) republics, all of them molded on the same pattern. It was, unhappily, often an uncongenial one, forced upon them by Napoleonic oversimplification coupled with French rationalization.

The Cisalpine Republic, for example, was not even created in Italy. It was fashioned in Lyons on December 1, 1801. On that day, a Council of Lombard noblemen was summoned and in the absence of an Italian of sufficient stature, having the necessary qualifications and able to command the respect of powerful local factions, the presidency was conferred upon the First Consul. There was apparently no limit to the number of offices he could hold.

Monsiau's painting, a portion of which is reproduced below, shows the meeting in Lyons at which Napoleon (seated on the dais) was proclaimed President of the Cisalpine Republic. An Italian, Count Melzi d'Eril, of Milan, was appointed Vice President. This republic was made up of the former duchies of Modena, Parma and Milan and of the legations of Bologna and Ferrara and of Romagna. The Grand Duchy of Tuscany, which had been taken away from the Austrian Archduke John, was, with the addition of other lands, rechristened the Kingdom of Etruria (the heritage of the past was not to be lightly shaken off). Etruria was later to be ruled by a Spanish Infanta. Austria was thus almost completely ousted from Italy. Its last holding was Venetia, including Venice, up to the Adige.

THE FIRST CONSPIRACIES

Below, left, the attempt on Napoleon's life in the Rue Saint-Nicaise is shown in an anonymous print of the period. A barrel of explosives, concealed in a small wagon, was to have exploded when the First Consul's carriage went by. He was on his way to the opera on Christmas Eve, 1800. The explosion occurred as soon as Napoleon's carriage had gone by. There were 42 houses damaged, 22 persons killed and 57 wounded—none in any way connected with either Napoleon or politics. The Jacobins were blamed. One of the men taken and executed was the Italian sculptor Ceracchi, a childhood friend of Napoleon.

Dictatorship breeds resistance which in turn breeds plots and counterplots. The unfortunate immediate effect, if the plots fail, is to give the ruler an excuse for harsh measures of reprisals and repression. It was the plots hatched against him which were in great part responsible for the steadily growing personal power of Napoleon. The first and noisiest of these took place in the Rue Saint-Nicaise on Christmas Eve of 1800. There followed other conspiracies, some fomented by the English, which resulted in arrests, deportations and executions. The most dramatic one involved the Duc d'Enghien, a young Bourbon prince, cousin of the exiled rulers of France. In violation of Bavarian sovereignty he was kidnaped from Ettenheim, in the Duchy of Baden, where he was visiting his mistress, and brought back to France by a small military detachment. He was taken before a court-martial, tried for treason and summarily shot in the early hours of March 21, 1804, in the moat of the fortress of Vincennes. A lantern was placed beside him so that the firing squad could see where to aim. It is difficult to pinpoint Napoleon's part in the plot. Certainly the final political responsibility was his, and the murder did him incalculable damage.

One of the most famous conspiracies against Napoleon was the monarchist plot engineered by former General Pichegru and Georges Cadoudal, a former commander of the rebels in Brittany. The plot was the excuse for the arrest and execution of the Duc d'Enghien. Immediately below, the arrest of Pichegru, as shown in a contemporary engraving (he committed suicide in prison under suspicious circumstances in April, 1804). Below, center, the execution of Cadoudal in the Place de Gréve on June 24, 1804. Below, bottom, a contemporary royalist print showing the execution of the Duc d'Enghien, carried out clandestinely in the moat of the Château de Vincennes.

CORONATION
AT NOTRE DAME

Bonaparte had achieved a dictatorship for life; the next step was a hereditary monarchy. This was accomplished by the simple expedient of having the Senate declare him "Emperor of the French by the grace of God and the Constitutions of the Republic." The Senate vote took place on May 18, 1804. Shortly thereafter the usual plebiscite, with the usual overseas majority, sanctioned a *fait accompli*. On December 2, 1804, in the Cathedral of Notre Dame de Paris, the coronation ceremonies took place, blessed by Pope Pius VII, who had come from Rome. With the oath he took, the new emperor guaranteed to the people the privileges which the Revolution had gained for them, thus assuring himself the support of the vast majority of the French. Furthermore, the presence of the Pontiff himself conferred upon the newborn Empire a recognition which put it in the ranks of the ancient monarchies by divine right. But was peaceful coexistence possible between a monarchy, offshoot of the Revolution, and other monarchies which had fought it? In the noisy celebrations, no one asked the question. However, it was soon evident that a French peace was no longer sufficient; it was an imperial peace that was required. And so the fires of war were rekindled.

To the left:
Napoleon as Emperor, by Gérard.
Napoleon, as Emperor,
wanted all the pomp and
circumstance he could command,
for he realized its appeal
to the masses. As soon as he
had been proclaimed Emperor,
he lost no time in setting up a
court like other royal courts. His
family became a dynasty of
"French Princes" while he gathered
about him "Grand Dignitaries"
with high-sounding titles: "Grand
Electors"; the "Arch-Chancellors of
the Empire, of State"; the "Arch-
Treasurer" the "Connétable," the
"Grand Admiral." Among the
"Grand Military officials" there
were fourteen "Imperial Marshals."
He turned state occasions
into great public shows. Typical

of these was his coronation.
Among its major features were the
heavy cloaks (the Empress Joséphine
staggered under the weight of hers
as she approached the altar) and
the sumptuous trappings of royalty.
The painter David, a former member
of the Convention who had voted for
the death of the king, became the
Empire's official painter.
His famous painting (above)
shows Napoleon as he is about to
place the crown on his wife's head.
The painting originally showed
Pope Pius VII with his hands in
his lap. Napoleon suggested to
David, long after the ceremony,
that the Pope's portrait be altered
to show his hand raised in
a benediction; otherwise, he
pointed out, what was the
purpose of his being there?

Below: two episodes in the Campaign of 1805: the surrender of the Austrians at Ulm, as depicted by Thévenin, and the battle of Elchingen, near Ulm, in Bavaria. Here on October 14, 1805 the forces under the command of Ney cut off the Austrians' retreat to the north, thus forcing them to surrender six days later. 50,000 prisoners fell into the trap. The credit for these spectacular victories belongs to the "Grande Armée," which had originally been assembled for the invasion of England. It was destined to achieve great fame with its grenadier guards and its troops of light infantry.

At the right: The lithographs made by Charlet, the son of a soldier of the Republican armies, were very popular, as were those by Raffet, whose drawings of the soldiers of Napoleon were unequaled in quality and number.

Below, a view of the roadway of the port of Boulogne (on the English Channel) where Napoleon concentrated his Grande Armée shortly after it had been formed, presumably to invade England. Below this, Boilly's picture of the reading of one of the bulletins on the activities of the Grande Armée, this one on the capitulation of Ulm. These bulletins were most effective instruments of propaganda.

DEATH AND VICTORY OF NELSON

On October 21, 1805, one day after the defeat at Ulm of General Mack, the commander of the Austrian forces, Lord Nelson defeated the Franco-Spanish fleet off Cape Trafalgar, near the northwest shore of the Strait of Gibraltar.
The treaty of Amiens had brought only a year's respite in a struggle that was to continue until the fall of the Empire. England, safe on her side of the Channel now that Napoleon had given up his plan to invade her, felt few repercussions of this struggle. Napoleon ordered Admiral Villeneuve to Brest in Brittany, but the latter, judging correctly that in the transfer to Germany of the troops that had been massed in Boulogne, the invasion scheme had been abandoned, sailed south instead to the Atlantic port of Cadiz. This move aroused the imperial wrath and the order to set sail at once for the Mediterranean. The order simplified Nelson's task, for his first concern had been to lure Villeneuve to put to sea. The latter, although still smarting from his defeat seven years earlier at the Battle of the Nile, had no choice but to obey. Nelson, on the other hand, was entirely free to maneuver. His ships closed in on the Franco-Spanish fleet, and six hours later, struck by a French bullet, he lay dying, but he had won the battle. Eighteen of the 33 enemy ships had been put out of commission, and the greatest naval battle in history was over. England could boast of still being mistress of the seas.

34

THE BRIGHT SUN OF AUSTERLITZ

Below, two highlights in the campaign of 1805, before Austerlitz. In Meynier's painting immediately below, Marshal Ney returns to the 76th Line Regiment their banners, lost in Italy in 1799 and located by him in the Innsbruck Arsenal. The painting was commissioned by the Emperor. Ney, who with his troops had been detached from the Grande Armée, ousted Archduke John from the Tyrol. Having taken Schnarwitz on November 7, he entered Innsbruck as the Austrian Archduke fell back on Klagenfurt. In Girodet's painting at the bottom of the page, Napoleon is receiving the keys to the City of Vienna on November 13, 1805.

The campaign of 1805 against what came to be known as the third coalition, England, Austria, Russia, against Napoleon, was conducted with breath-taking speed and efficiency. Its seeds had been sown during the brief peace which lasted from 1801 to 1802, at which date hostilities were resumed, this time by England over the interpretation of the Treaty of Amiens. The three years directly following saw profound changes in the political and geographic face of Western Europe. Napoleon had become Mediator of the Swiss Confederation and President of the Italian Republic, which had been rechristened the Cisalpine Republic. Piedmont, Elba and Genoa had been annexed by France and the Neapolitan ports were occupied by her as well.

But it was Germany that witnessed the most revolutionary and far-reaching consequences of that short-lived peace. Besides occupying the port of Hamburg and Hannover, of which George III was Elector, Napoleon set to work reducing the number of small German states from roughly 300 to 83. He also distributed some of the Hapsburgs' German holdings among Prussia, Bavaria and Würtemberg. As for the Italian Republic, as France had become an empire, it also changed its name and became the Kingdom of Italy, with Napoleon no longer its president but its king, duly self-crowned.

However, the members of the coalition did not always see eye to eye. The two principal partners were the Austrian Emperor and the Russian Csar; England was a passionately interested party and Prussia was already switching from side to side when it was not actually double-dealing. Csar Alexander I, who had only recently inherited the throne from his father, Paul I (to whose assassination he may well have given his tacit consent, if he had not actually taken an active part in it) had aroused great moral indignation against Napoleon by loudly and sanctimoniously deploring the murder of the Duc d'Enghien. In those days also questions of morality had an effect on political ones. The Austrian Emperor Francis II had joined the coalition only in August. Napoleon, having abandoned his scheme for the invasion of England, conducted what would today be described as a preventive war. After a first clash in Bavaria in October, the campaign was brought to a close on the Moravian hills. The battle took place on a field near Austerlitz on a cold, cloudless day, December 2, 1805, the first anniversary of his coronation. That brilliant winter sun became for a time the symbol of Napoleon's bright fortunes.

General Lejeune's painting below, of the bivouac on the eve of the battle of Austerlitz, was exhibited at the Paris Salon of 1808 where it won a prize. The Emperor with an escort carrying lighted torches, spent the night with his soldiers, visiting outposts. His arrival was like a signal: the soldiers on watch snatched up straw which they fashioned into crude torches, and a whole succession of small fires, the famous "bivouac fires of Austerlitz," were lit. Napoleon had cleared out of the small village of Austerlitz on November 29 and encamped on a plain nearby. The Austro-Russian forces, thinking to cut the French off from Vienna, tried to surround him.

The name "Austerlitz" does not appear on modern maps. The small village has not disappeared—it's simply that it has changed names. Its Slavic name is Slavkov u Brna, a small town with a population of 4,500, impervious to past glories. The battle itself remains one of the tactical masterpieces of Napoleonic strategy. It unfolded precisely as he had foreseen that it would. It proceeded exactly as if he had radioed instructions to the enemy commanders, or as if through some mysterious and still uninvented device he had managed to read their minds, hour by hour. He himself had selected the

terrain 10 days before the battle.
He had headed toward the north
while the Austro-Russian forces
were meeting in Moravia.
The enemy thought they would cut
off his retreat on Vienna
and thus they fell into the trap
he had set for them. The battle,
begun with the first rays of the dawn
on December 2, was finished by
sunset of that short winter day—
4 p.m. The Austro-Russians
lost at least 35,000 men,
50 banners, and almost all their
cannons, which were subsequently
melted down to erect, in Paris,
the Colonne Vendôme. The victory
had cost Napoleon 8,000 men,
1,300 of whom had been killed.
Gérard's painting, below,
shows the epilogue of the
battle: in the foreground,
Napoleon, surrounded by his
General Staff, is approached
from the left by General Rapp,
hatless. Behind him, in the
white tunic of the soldiers
of the Austrian Emperor,
is Prince Repnin, who
had been taken prisoner.

In the print: **LA PAIX** GRACE *L'IMMORTEL* NAPOLEON

C'est moi Messieurs les Français, qui vous offre les meilleures étrennes.

To the left, a print from the Hennin collection. Street criers had returned to the public squares holding their audiences spellbound with the news of the peace signed at Pressburg on December 26, 1805. Peace at last, thanks to Napoleon. "Mine is the greatest gift to you." This was perhaps the happiest moment during the whole of the empire.

To the right, above, Prud'hon's painting of the meeting, on December 6, 1805, between Napoleon and Francis II. This was the first meeting between the heads of the two empires—the Holy Roman Empire, which had been neither holy nor Roman for some time, and the new French Empire, which aspired to remold Europe. Vernet's painting, far right, shows Napoleon at Jena, after the resumption of hostilities. He is startled by the remarks of a grenadier. The campaign in Saxony put the Prussians out of commission. This very brief campaign came to an end on October 27, 1806, when Napoleon entered Berlin. He is shown doing so, center-right illustration, surrounded by a spectacular retinue.

Next came the Polish campaign against the Russians. Below, left, the battle of Eylau as seen by Baron Legros. The painting won a prize in an exhibit sponsored by Napoleon. He himself had suggested the subject: a warning about the horrors of war. The artist painted him as he was supposed to be saying, "If other rulers could see this, they would be less eager for war and conquests."

Bottom, right, Vernet's painting of the battle of Friedland: Napoleon is surrounded by some of his marshals: Ney, Nansouty and Oudinot; in the left foreground, the body of a dead Russian general lying close by his cannons.

The peace imposed upon Austria at Pressburg had given Venetia back to the Kingdom of Italy, taken Istria and Dalmatia from the Austrians, enlarged Bavaria and the Tyrol—in short, ousted Austria from Germany and Italy. Prussia, forced to accept the French alliance, took back Hannover but lost the chance to serve as mediator between the east and the west. However, at the earliest opportunity, she switched sides again, letting Napoleon know that he had better clear out of the territories east of the Rhine. This was the beginning of the fourth coalition. Austria, busy licking her wounds, did not join in this time. A first campaign, in Saxony, lasted barely six days, from October 8 to 14, 1806, and put Prussia, defeated at Jena, out of commission. The second one, in Poland, lasted six months, half of it in the winter. After the inconclusive massacre at Eylau on February 8, 1807, Napoleon's victory at Friedland on June 14, induced Csar Alexander I of Russia to come to terms with the French, at the expense of Prussia, which had been reduced to four provinces.

Below, Gautherot's painting of the meeting between Napoleon and Csar Alexander I. This took place on June 25, 1807, at Tilsit on the Niemen River, on a barge specially built for the occasion. They both had their own retinues. The interview lasted almost two weeks, each putting himself out to charm and entertain the other. "The friendship between France and Russia has been my most cherished dream," Napoleon is supposed to have said to the Csar, who until then had made a point of referring to Napoleon as "General Bonaparte." A treaty of alliance sealed the new-found friendship between the two rulers.

LIFE DURING THE EMPIRE

Napoleon's empire left its imprint in many and varied fields: society, arts, economy, education, religion, administration. Its style in furniture gives a better flavor of life as it was lived during that period than many a book on the same subject. Originally sober and clean-cut in its neo-classic lines, it soon became ornate and fussy. With gilt heads and feet, of Egyptian inspiration, it degenerated into an absurdly overburdened style that was as uncomfortable to sit or recline on as it was heavy to move. Fashion took the same course; the simple classic draperies of the early period were soon added to with shawls, fringes and laces. But it was the men who reached the height of the absurd with pantaloons so tight that it was impossible to sit down and collars so high and stiff that it was impossible to bend the neck or look sideways.

Like all great propagandists, Napoleon realized the importance of outward form, or as today's public-relations men would put it, of the image created. Pomp and circumstance were essential, witness the elaborate coronation ceremonies and the festivities attending the birth of the King of Rome.

Napoleon had also created a new society by resurrecting titles of nobility for a new aristocracy, based on merit, whose titles were culled from victories or from new lands acquired by the Empire. Most of the titles were hereditary, but had Napoleon lasted, the ranks of the new nobility would have remained open to new talent. The newcomers were not only soldiers, they were administrators, scientists, artists, professional men. Talent was rewarded and safely placed under government control. Even before assuming the title of Emperor he had founded, in 1802, the Legion of Honor, whose members were chosen for meritorious service. Unlike other ancient orders of chivalry, it was a hierarchy, with five ranks. The marshals he appointed were called Marshals of the Empire, not just of France. And the new elite that had come into being was rewarded with a generosity unparalleled in the annals of history. Napoleon believed a bit simple-mindedly that devotion could be bought with gold. Besides the large emoluments that went with certain offices there were also considerable "fringe benefits." Talleyrand was the happy recipient, until he fell from grace, of an annual sum of 495,000 francs; Marshal Berthier, of 1,300,000.

He was also careful to woo the masses, and for a long time succeeded in retaining their loyalty. Once order had been established, the common people were able to enjoy the fruits of the Revolution. No matter how badly they were paid, tenant farmers and laborers were at least able to live off the land. Except in big cities, the cost of living was low, especially in towns and villages where local produce was available. With an annual income of 600 francs it was possible, in Alsace, for example, to live in relative comfort. The increase in the consumption of wine and meat was a clear indication of the improved standard of living. Grain harvests were abundant until 1810, and cattle breeding was continually improving.

The economy was also thriving. At the beginning of the Empire, France had been primarily an agricultural nation; the creation through her conquests and territorial annexations of a larger market for her goods encouraged industrial development. Even the continental blockade against England encouraged the French economy in that it spurred the cultivation of new food products and the research and development of substitutes. The cultivation of potatoes, which had been virtually unknown in Europe until then, became widespread, while in the north of France, the cultivation of chicory as a substitute for coffee, became prevalent. But the piece of research that had the most profitable and far-reaching consequences was the discovery that sugar could be extracted from beets as well as from sugar cane. To be sure, the Germans had been the first to develop this, but it was the French who perfected the technique so that the production of sugar ultimately became a major industry. Fairs, exhibitions and state subsidies helped all forms of industry.

New impetus was given to textiles, and the steel industry made great strides forward. For the first time in Paris, great metal structures were put up: the Pont des Arts in 1803 over the Seine, the cupola of the Grain Market in 1811. Toward the end of the Empire, in 1813, France had achieved an almost perfectly balanced economy: the industrial output was of one billion four hundred million francs; the agricultural output one billion six hundred million francs.

Napoleon, a great believer in centralized control, was interested in every phase of the nation's growth and kept himself informed of every new development. He distributed prizes right and left, encouraged, visited, criticized. He took a personal interest in great public works, caused ports like Cherbourg to be enlarged and had new ones, such as Antwerp, built; he ordered the digging of navigable canals, thus linking all of France through waterways. And, above all, he set up a network of major roads which connected the coastal roads of the Mediterranean to those beyond the Alps.

Wanting to make of Paris, whose population had increased from 548,000 in 1802 to 650,000 in 1814, a capital worthy of his empire, he commissioned his favorite architects to build monuments calculated to increase the prestige of the nation like the Column of the *Grande Armée* in the Place Vendôme, the Arch of Triumph. It was during his reign also that three of the bridges over the Seine were built, the previously mentioned Pont des Arts and the two named after victories, Austerlitz and Jena.

All this required money, a great deal of money. True, the Court of Accounts, which he had set up, kept a watchful eye on the spending of public funds while the creation of the Bank of France stabilized the currency. But the greatest expenses incurred were for wars. These were met only in part by what today would be called "reparations." In the long run it was the wars which ruined the Empire. One of the most expensive ones had been the war in Spain, which in six years swallowed up 350 million francs.

The constant movement of troops also changed the direction of the traditional currents of European traffic. In the past they had been directed from north to south; they were redirected to go from west to east.

There were times, inevitably, when a machine as complex as the one put into motion by Napoleon would miss a stroke or spin on its wheels. Napoleon was a better innovator than curator. Always impatient for change—which was not always synonymous with improvement—he would destroy in a few days what it had taken him years to build up. He would set up a system and then act as though he didn't believe in it. He wanted collaborators and yet trusted only servants who, like their kind from the beginning of time, eventually betrayed their master.

However, the centralized structure he set up in France was destined to outlive him just as the school system he had devised outlived him. He was the real founder, in Europe, of the lay state, for it was he who actually enforced the separation of Church and State. He made the major mistake of trying to have the State control the Church, but this did not detract from the basic accomplishment.

Were people happy under Napoleon? The question is a natural one. Why shouldn't they have been, so long as the winds of glory swelled the sails of the imperial ship? True, the intellectuals could bemoan a censorship that became increasingly petty and inclusive (which is after all the essence of censorship); his past and future foes could bemoan a police that became increasingly brutal and arbitrary (like so many police forces), but hardly anyone, except the die-hards, regretted the old order wiped out by the Revolution and from whose ruins had sprung the new order.

Some, who had stayed home, had made out very well, profiteering, consolidating their positions and enjoying life to the hilt. Others, first among whom were the soldiers of the *Grande Armée*, rejoiced and basked in the reflected glory of the Empire, never stinting their sacrifices, since honors and booty were their reward. When they returned home between campaigns they could show off their glittering and exuberant uniforms, their glistening helmets. Some of them even received titles along with their decorations. War was perhaps inconvenient, but it was also glamorous. One of the most popular pastimes of the era was dancing. A mania for it had swept over the country, in all walks of life, from the common people dancing in the streets to celebrate a victory, to the aristocracy with their swanlike beauties waltzing with dashing military men. Between the two extremes were the bourgeois and the inevitably numerous *nouveaux riches* who hired halls, gardens, even disused convents for the purpose.

REVOLUTION WITHOUT END

To the left is David's portrait of the Emperor in 1810 when he has just crossed the threshold of 40. He is wearing his favorite uniform, that of a colonel of the guard. A comparison with his portrait as First Consul, on page 20, will show the great changes that have taken place within a decade. Not only have his thinning hair and increased girth aged him, but the whole picture is that of a man grown old before his time. Michelet used to say of this painting that David had proven himself to be "conscientious, courageous, free from complacency, interested only in the truth." And to be sure, the years had not dealt kindly with Napoleon. This may have been caused by the peptic ulcer from which he was already suffering and which in time became cancerous. (His father had died at an early age of this same ailment). But his rapid aging was undoubtedly due in major part to the weight of the power he wielded, for nothing wears down so much as absolute power.

By 1806 the Revolutionary calendar, which had lasted some 14 years, had already become superannuated and the word "Republic" had disappeared from everyday use. Two years later the word also vanished from the currency. But the Revolution had not stopped; its impetus had been such that it had to go on, and its chief surviving protagonist continued to direct all his energies to organizing and uniting a Europe that was often reluctant and more often openly hostile. But despite this resistance, something of his imperial system survived; the nationalism and individualism that he tried to suppress were actually rekindled and reanimated by the repressive measures he had taken. His glory, built upon the sands of military victories, began to fade in the twilight brought on by the burdens of war, and his hold on the peoples of Europe weakened; but the seeds of revolution were sown, and his brief rule showed the people what an efficient administration could accomplish for them.

THE SPANISH DEBACLE

Goya's famous painting of the Second of May is one of the most impressive documents of the Spanish war. In a nightmarish light, it depicts the savage reprisals ordered by Murat for a popular uprising in Madrid on May 2, 1808. The revolt had broken out unexpectedly. Rumor had spread that the French were about to arrest the last prince of the ruling house, who had remained in Madrid. During that very night, a number of citizens of Madrid, including some monks, were summarily executed. This was the spark that set off the unquenchable fires of insurrection.

Immediately below, a painting by Charles Vernet which hangs in the museum at Versailles. It shows Napoleon on December 4, 1808, demanding the surrender of the Spanish capital. Standing next to him is Marshal Duroc, Duke of Friuli, who shows his watch and points out that the envoys from the Spanish capital will be executed if the city has not surrendered within one hour.

Below this, a contemporary print of the battle of Vitoria. Here Wellington attacked Joseph Bonaparte, forcing him back beyond the Pyrenees. After the fall of the Empire, Joseph emigrated to the United States, where he lived from 1815 to 1841. He then returned to Europe to take up residence in Florence, where he died in 1844. He was born in 1768.

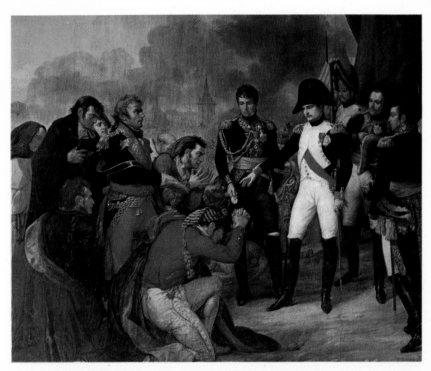

Twice Nelson's England had defeated Napoleon on the seas; the first time at the Battle of the Nile, the second time at Trafalgar. Several times England had succeeded in pitting some monarch or other against him, always giving an encouraging hand to the coalition against him. But never yet had she succeeded in loosening his hold on the continent. Her much-touted supremacy on the seas was all very well, but it wasn't enough. The *Grand Empire* which was the direct result of the *Grande Armée* was growing continually, and it looked, after Tilsit, as though nothing could stop it. But the Spaniards did.

The tide turned when, with the deposition of the inept Bourbons in 1808, Napoleon transferred his brother Joseph from Naples to the Spanish throne, just as one might transfer any insignificant official from one post to another. But this time things did not go as usual. The Spaniards wanted no part of the "liberators," who had the bad habit of looting all the riches they could find, which in Spain meant in the churches. And thus it was that the *Grande Armée* found itself confronting an enemy as implacable as it was elusive, inflamed with patriotism and religious ardor, fighting its own war of liberation which it also looked upon as a crusade. Bailén, on July 23, 1808, where 18,000 French troops put down their arms before the Spaniards, was more than just a signal of alarm: It was the end of a myth, the myth of Napoleon's invulnerability. Entering Madrid on December 5, 1808, Napoleon thought he had regained the upper hand. He was wrong: It was a partisan war being fought by men who did not understand peace; all they wanted was the end of the enemy. And it swallowed up 300,000 men of the *Grande Armée*.

Furthermore, one small and at first insignificant fact emerged, a small white cloud which in time would grow into a black storm; the Spanish undertaking opened up to England that "second front" which the supremacy of the seas had not been enough to give her. On August 1, 1808, a small corps consisting of 15,000 soldiers under the command of Arthur Wellesley, Duke of Wellington (1769–1852) landed in Portugal, whence it moved into Spain. It was to stop only six years later, in 1814, on French territory, at Toulon. These troops were numerically negligible, but there are times in history when numbers do not necessarily mean strength.

47

EMPTY VICTORIES

Four years had passed since the sun had risen on Austerlitz. From victory to victory, condemned for life to the pursuit of his own glory, Napoleon continued to chase after an elusive peace. The next outbreak of war came from Austria, who had made herself the champion of the German people, this even though her emperor had lost his German possessions. It was strange indeed to find the heir to the Hapsburgs throwing a protective mantle over Germany.

Napoleon managed to defeat his opponents once more by the speed with which he could strike. Between the 19th and the 23rd of April, in five days, he divided the Austrian forces. This time, however, they were undaunted. He tried to force his way across the Danube at Aspern and at Essling, but on May 22 he was held in check, driven back to his starting point and forced to entrench himself in the small island of Lobau. Both sides suffered heavy losses, more noticeable to Napoleon, for he had lost some of his best men in the battle, including Lannes, one of his favorite marshals. But he did not give in to the pleas of his commanding officers to retire; instead he called in all the reinforcements he could muster, and in two days of battle, July 5–6, he won at Wagram. Victory was his once more, though this time it was slower in coming, for it had been a difficult battle.

Austria, discouraged by her inability to defeat Napoleon, asked for peace. She obtained it with the Treaty of Vienna on October 14, 1809, through the harsh terms of which she was forced to give up more territories and reduce the size of her army. Napoleon also began the negotiations for his marriage to an Austrian Archduchess, Marie Louise, daughter of the Emperor Francis II.

Meantime there had been other threats against the *Grand Empire*. In the Tyrol an innkeeper, Andrea Hofer, led a revolt of 20,000 peasants against their Bavarian oppressors. Hofer refused to recognize the armistice that had been signed after Wagram and disregarded the Peace Treaty of Vienna. The French joined the Bavarians and finally succeeded in quelling the insurrection, which had lasted from April to December, 1809, but only after the treacherous capture, and execution, of their leader.

There was further trouble; two days before the signing of the treaty a young Saxon student, son of a clergyman, tried to stab Napoleon because, as he told the Emperor, who questioned him, Napoleon was the incarnation of misfortune for his country.

While these events were taking place, the English had finally achieved a landing on the island of Walcheren in the Netherlands. Their success, it is true, was short-lived, for they were soon forced to re-embark. But it was another straw in the wind. The bright sunlight of Austerlitz was beginning to fade.

To the left, a painting by Gautherot of Napoleon at Ratisbon. This was the second time he was wounded on the field of battle. Many years before, he had been stabbed in the chest by a bayonet at the siege of Toulon. This time the bullet grazed his right heel. His Achilles' heel? Below, Archduke Charles of Austria during the battle of Essling on May 22, when Napoleon's troops were thrown back to the Danube. Bottom of the page, Horace Vernet's painting, in the Versailles museum, of Napoleon directing the battle of Wagram. The revenge for the near defeat at Aspern and Essling was preceded, on the night of July 4 to 5, by the fording of the Danube to the island of Lobau, south of Essling, in a maneuver which took the enemy by surprise. Below, right, Napoleon's return to the island of Lobau as seen by Meynier. This painting, which hangs in the museum at Versailles, points up the desperate plight of the French forces.

Every possible type of soldier in the Grande Armée and the legendary but real comradeship that existed between the "Petit Caporal," as Napoleon was affectionately known, and his men were the subjects of endless drawings in the Napoleonic era. Many have already been reproduced in this volume, especially those by Raffet. Below in three lithographs by Charlet and Bellangé

are shown a few characteristic traits of the "Jean-Jean" and the "Dumanet" as the new recuits and the veterans of the imperial armies were jokingly called. Old hands and young ones, in their friendly rivalry, were animated by the same esprit de corps. They had an almost fanatic reverence for the Emperor. The "grumblers" of the Old Guard all addressed him with great familiarity.

The Republic had had a number of separate armies, each of which bore the name of its theater of operations. They were the armies of the Rhine, of the Sambre and Meuse, of Italy, and so forth. Even before he had become Emperor, Napoleon had made profound changes in this setup. There came into being one single army, the *Grande Armée*. The name at first signified that it was a numerically large army, a single one as opposed to the other small, fragmentary ones. Another reason for unification, of course, was the possible eventual need to protect by armed force a regime that had been set up in that very manner. There would be no danger of a military coup if the loyalty of all the officers had been pledged to the Emperor.

Consequently the "*Grande Armée*" and the "*Grand Empire*" became the two sides of the same medal. The *Grande Armée* was divided into corps, brigades and divisions. Its elite were the Imperial Guard, another of Napoleon's creations, a corps of hand-picked, seasoned troops, a kind of personal army at the heart of the imperial army.

As the Napoleonic Empire was gradually evolving into a European system, the *Grande Armée* also changed aspect, continually taking on contingents that were not French. Of the 700,000 men who were in arms at the start of the Russian campaign, only 300,000, including the Guards, were French. The other 400,000 were, in varying proportions, German, Polish, Lithuanian, Italian and even Spanish and Portuguese. It was naturally they who suffered the greatest losses in the disastrous retreat from Moscow.

Napoleon's era was one that believed devoutly in the glories of military life and in romantic if hazardous feats of arms, so the Emperor exploited to the utmost his soldiers' burning desire to distinguish themselves on the field of battle. He developed to a fine art the "cult of personality," for he had been able to instill a fanatic devotion to himself in the greater part of his army, even among the foreign elements. The deep attachment of his soldiers was not a gratuitous invention nor a posthumous legend; it was a reality which continued as long as his victories lasted and in some cases lived on after his fall and death. It was a factor with which his enemies both at home and abroad had to contend.

REPUDIATION OF THE BEAUTIFUL JOSEPHINE

In mid-December, 1809, in a quiet ceremony which lasted about half an hour, the final divorce decree between Napoleon and Joséphine was signed. The decision, which had certainly been the chief topic of gossip for many months, was announced formally by the Emperor to the Empress on November 30 during a private meeting at the Tuileries Palace. According to the eyewitness account of Bausset, the palace prefect, Joséphine fainted, although the announcement cannot have been unexpected. When Bausset, summoned by the Emperor, lifted her to carry her to her apartments, the lady whispered to him: "You're hurting me; don't hold me so tight." Below, Chasselat's interpretation of the scene.

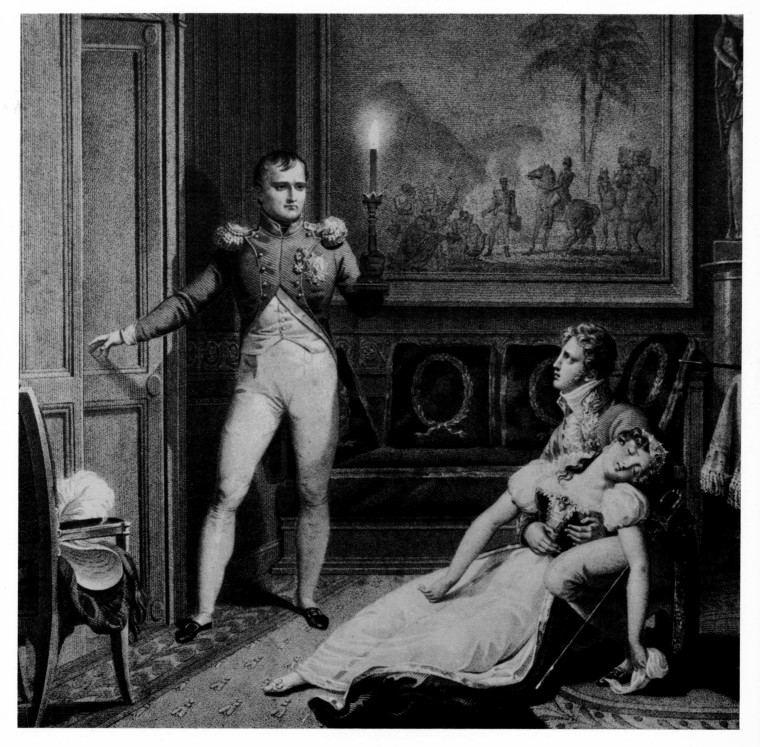

THE NEW FAMILY

Napoleon could see no point in the creation of a hereditary Empire if there was no heir. Certain that the responsibility for the sterility of their marriage was entirely Joséphine's, he set in motion the preparations for another marriage, this one dictated by reasons of state. The bride chosen was the Archduchess of Austria, Marie Louise, daughter of the Emperor Francis II. There was a feeling of unease in the air when it was learned that another Austrian princess was to be imported. The last one, married to Louis XVI, had been decidedly unlucky for France, not to mention for herself, her son and her husband. The 18-year-old bride was solemnly married off in one of the last great ceremonies staged by the Empire, which had then reached the zenith of its territorial and political expansion.

The bond between the latest comer in the assembly of kings and the most ancient and proud ruling house of old Europe was sealed by the birth, on March 20, 1811, of the King of Rome, heir to the imperial throne. With a new family all his own, Napoleon could at last cast off the thralldom of his old family ties, brothers and sisters, who were never satisfied with the crowns and retinues bestowed upon them by a generous older brother whose chief mistake had apparently been that he put them in positions to which they themselves could never have even aspired.

Opposite, Rouget's painting of the wedding of Napoleon and Marie Louise, celebrated in Paris on April 1, 1810. Rouget, a pupil of David, was far from equaling his master. Above, Napoleon and his son in a painting attributed to Steuben. Below, from left to right, Napoleon's four brothers: Louis, King of Netherlands; Jerome, King of Westphalia; Joseph (the eldest), King of Spain; Lucien, who had paved the way for the coup d'état of the 18 Brumaire.

RUSSIAN SNOWS BURY THE GRANDE ARMÉE

It is the privilege of posterity to pronounce judgment on men's actions. Napoleon's have given rise to innumerable contradictory verdicts. However, historians agree unanimously that the Russian campaign undertaken in June, 1812, was his second major blunder, the first one being the Spanish campaign four years earlier. Was the Russian blunder the determining factor in the fall of Napoleon? Was it irreparable? Could he have avoided altogether making the mistake? The answer to the first question is yes. It was decisive because he maimed beyond repair his own army, losing more than half of it on the frozen Russian fields and rivers. At the conclusion of his retreat he was left with only a handful of the *Grande Armée*, the instrument without which the *Grand Empire* would inevitably crumble. And this answers the second question as well. That the error was avoidable is a matter of conjecture.

One thing is certain, however. Napoleon's mania for setting everything in order, and to do so in a hurry, was at the base of his desire to reactivate his alliance of friendship with Csar Alexander. Twice the two had come to an understanding, first at Tilsit, then at Erfurt in a meeting which had lasted from September 27 to October 14, 1808. But this was not enough to reconcile their basic differences. In order to perpetuate a Napoleonic Europe, it was essential to expel from it Holy and Imperial Russia, to thrust it back farther to the east. This was all the more necessary because the Spanish game was still being played against England. She had gained a foothold in the Iberian peninsula, thus forming a second front that was as yet only embryonic but still growing. The Franco-Russian Alliance was a living corpse that poisoned the air. It was, in a sense, similar to the semi-alliance of the Germans and the Russians almost a century and a half later. The entente between Napoleon and Alexander had been concluded with each one's tacit understanding that the other's hands would be tied and that he himself could use it to consolidate his own position. For this reason Napoleon thought it essential to renegotiate an entente, the terms of which he would dictate after having brilliantly defeated his "friend" in one or two battles. It had not occurred to him that in addition to the Russian army he would have to fight the Russian people.

It was on August 15, 1812, the anniversary of the founding of the Empire and Napoleon's birthday, that the future of the Russian campaign was decided, at Smolensk. Napoleon's troops crossed the Dnieper River. Napoleon decided on the 17th to take the city while the Russians withdrew. See painting opposite.

The Russians were defeated at Borodino on the Moskva River directly below on September 7, 1812, but it was less than a defeat, more of a stalemate, for the Russians retired in good order. When on September 13 Napoleon entered Moscow, he found the city deserted and in flames. He was forced to abandon it.

(below left) And so in October began the retreat which turned into a disaster with the crossing, November 25th to 29th, of the Berezina River. The heroic episodes, the sacrifices of the war-weary rear guard, the desperate last-ditch stands were all in vain.

The tragedy of the Grande Armée and of the retreat during which it lost 380,000 men, including most of the Guard which had been reduced from 30,000 men to a paltry 1,500, is depicted in numerous prints and lithographs. Below, two of the most poignant. The first one shows Napoleon's melancholy return. The second one, below, shows an old grenadier as he buries a flag to keep it from falling into enemy hands. The retreat had started on Saturday, October 19, 1812. The remains of the army, decimated by the freezing weather and attacks by the Cossacks, reached the Berezina River, which marked the Russian boundary, on November 25, 1812.

At one point during the Second World War when Germany was headed straight for disaster, a group of the military decided to get rid of Hitler; this was the Generals' Plot of July 20, 1944. Something similar took place in Napoleon's time. The first attempt to oust him from the inside came from the army. While the Emperor was still in Russia, a general with republican ideas, Malet, tried a coup. He announced that Napoleon had been killed, arrested the ministers of war and police and set up a provisional government in Paris. This happened during the night of October 23 to 24, 1812.

General Malet's plot was unmasked, he was tried summarily, and duly executed. The episode was short-lived, but it was disquieting for two reasons. First, because the coup had been engineered by a soldier, and the Empire was a military structure; second, because no one had remembered that there was not only a legitimate heir but his mother also. The dynasty was demonstrably very fragile. There were other portents within France, but there were even more of them outside. The cement of victory had begun to crack.

Napoleon found that he was being called to account for his actions not only by his former allies and future enemies but by the masses of people whom he had tried to rule under a single flag. They had not fully understood to what extent the Empire was European. Napoleon's forcing them to unite had only served to awaken in them the seeds of nationalism and to strengthen their resistance. This had already happened in Spain; it did so in Prussia, which felt itself to be not only anti-French but basically German, so that it took over the leadership of pan-Germanism from Austria. There were many others who were ready to attack the frontiers, while at home there grew a clique which was getting ready to "salvage the salvageable," which involved ousting Napoleon.

Worried by these reports from home, Napoleon secretly left the retreating army on December 5, 1812, before its arrival in Vilno, and hastened back to Paris. His unexpected return had only one thing in common with his precipitate return so many years before from Egypt. In both cases, the news from home had been disquieting; everything then had also been at stake, but everything remained to be done; this time the stakes were as great, but too much had already been done.

STILL THE PEOPLE TRUST IN HIM

The Emperor's popularity remained intact, or almost so, among the common people, who were not yet prepared to renounce glory even though they paid for it so dearly. Bellangé's print, below, is significant. The peasant, pointing to a picture of the Emperor, says to the parish priest: "For me, he will always be Our Father."

THE BOYS
OF THE
SAXON CAMPAIGN

If the story Prince Metternich tells is true, and there is no reason to doubt him, it seems that having been sent by Emperor Francis II to meet Napoleon at Dresden on June 26, 1813, he was told by the French Emperor, "Two weeks ago I could still have made peace; today I cannot. I have won two battles. I shall not make peace." The two battles to which he was referring were the battles of Lützen (May 1–2) and Bautzen (May 19, 1813) during the Saxon campaign against the Russians and the Prussians. These latter had upset operations on the front first with the passage to the other side of General York, commander of the Prussian auxiliary corps in the Imperial Army, then with the direct appeal "To my people"—the formula itself was new—of King Frederick William, who was proclaiming his own "war of liberation."

The two battles to which Napoleon referred were important not in themselves but for the tragic realization they brought to him. "I can't make peace because I am winning." This was to be henceforth the heart of the matter. Napoleon was more than ever the captive of his victories and of himself. He had already in the past said something similar but, repeated at this juncture, it sounded like a confession.

It was now impossible to put a number to the coalitions that formed against him. The last one, which came into being after a three-month armistice, was known as the General Coalition. After an initial hesitation, Austria had secretly signed a pact with Russia and Prussia and had again entered the field of battle. Napoleon had hoped till the last for the nonintervention of Austria. Despite the disquieting news from Spain, where Wellington had entered Madrid and had won a battle at Vitoria, the Emperor was convinced he could still win. But this time the game was too big, even for him. All his enemies, old and new, had entered the lists: Russia, Prussia, Austria, with England as usual, not to mention all the minor partners. The Europe of the Empire had reached its epilogue.

All of Europe, not only the Europe of princes, was rebelling against the man who had wanted to unite it at all costs, against the man who had tried in vain to make it European.

The army which had been put on the battlefield by Napoleon once more the General rather than the Emperor was made up in great part of young, very young recruits. During the campaign in Saxony, and later, in France, they were known as the "Marie Louises," a nickname that had overtones of affection rather than scorn. Two of them are shown, opposite, in a picture by Raffet.

After having lost half a million men, Napoleon had succeeded, miraculously, in putting together another 300,000. But although courage and devotion were not lacking, these were of an entirely different caliber. The Germans had rechristened the battle of Leipzig the "Battle of Nations" in which Napoleon with 150,000 men,

driven against the Elster River, withstood for three days—October 16–18—the onslaught of the United forces of Russia, Prussia and Austria who were 300,000 men strong. But it was mainly a battle of princes. Below, the meeting of the sovereigns as the Prince of Schwarzenberg brings them the news of the victory.

FRANCE INVADED!

Below, two moments in Napoleon's last battles in the defense of France, invaded by the enemy. The first one, a lithograph by Bellangé, titled Long Live the Emperor, shows the battle at Montmirail on February 11, 1814. The second one, a lithograph by Lavigne, shows the battle at Montereau, where Napoleon on February 18 had beaten the Prussians under Blücher, but was unable to make the most of his initial successes. Opposite: Horace Vernet's painting of the last unsuccessful defense of Paris at the gates of Clichy. The troops were under the command of Marshal Moncey. Among those who took part in the battle were members of the National Guard, volunteers, graduates of the famous Ecole Polytechnique founded by Napoleon.

And so Napoleon was forced once more, in his own words, "to pull on the boots of the General of the Army in Italy." But in those tumultuous 15 years since the words were first spoken, his foot had grown larger, and those boots had become too tight. Having lost Germany, Napoleon had tried to gain time and to put a brake on the centrifugal force that was already making the Empire disintegrate. The "Allies," as they were now generally known, had, according to them, made use of that time of waiting to strengthen military pressure with political action and propaganda. The leaflets distributed by them told the French that they had no quarrel with them, only with Napoleon. The invitation was clear: Get rid of him, and we'll leave you alone. The appeal had an odd ring, for it attached the label of "revolutionaries" and "liberators" to the sovereigns who had always ruled by divine right. These were adjectives which Napoleon and the French had once used to describe themselves, and they did now make some impression on those who were toying with the idea of "salvaging the salvageable." They were chiefly the ones who occupied the first rank of easy chairs.

Historians agree unanimously that the French campaign, from the beginning of the year 1814 to mid-March, was one of the masterpieces of Napoleon's strategy. But it was a series of hollow victories, and worthy of mention only because the campaign, victorious though it was, confirmed the truism that wars are not necessarily won on battlefields. The Allies had been convinced that they could easily defeat the 70,000 men, most of whom were conscripts, that Napoleon had managed to muster against them. They had planned to reach Paris within a week; it actually took them two months, with more than one disaster overtaking them. The Napoleonic speed of maneuvering, in a series of lightning thrusts, had put in jeopardy the fate of the coalition to such an extent that at Chaumont, on March 1, the Allies felt the need to reaffirm their pact to continue to the death the struggle against the "common enemy." At the last moment, Napoleon's bold plan of an eastward thrust to cut off the enemies' communications failed, partly through the defection of his own generals. The Allies, on March 31, 1814, entered Paris, empty of French troops.

Napoleon, forced by his marshals, abdicated on April 4 in favor of his son. Two days later he was again forced to abdicate, this time unconditionally.

The Farewell of Fountainbleau is the title of this famous painting by Horace Vernet. The Emperor had summoned together in the courtyard of the White Horse what remained of the Imperial Guard. The drums rolled. Then Napoleon signaled that he wanted to speak. He recalled to his old companions at arms the 20 years of glory that they had traveled together. He said that he had wanted to save France from the horrors of civil war. Summoning General Petit, with the standard flying the Imperial Eagle, he embraced him and the glorious banner, and added a few more words: "Let this last gesture remain in your hearts forever. Once more, good-bye, to you, my old comrades." It was a moving scene which inspired many poets, among them Byron. The author of this painting drew his inspiration from the story, as told by one of the eyewitnesses, Baron Fain. The characters are portrayed as they actually looked.

FAREWELL TO
THE IMPERIAL EAGLES!

The great adventure was over. Napoleon was leaving. The Allies allowed him to keep the title of Emperor, as though it were a medal or a decoration, and granted him a small patch of ground over which to rule: the island of Elba, which was halfway between a prison and an independent little state. It was, as a matter of fact, one of those numerous autonomous little states most of which Napoleon had wiped off the map of Europe.

Before he had even reached Elba, his successor Louis XVIII, brother of Louis XVI who had died on the guillotine, was already on his way back to France, following in the wake of "foreign bayonets" or, as some preferred to call them, "Allied Liberators." It had been decided by the Allies on April 11, 1814, that the French Government should pay Napoleon an annual income of two million francs—a compromise between a bribe and a pension.

There are still many pages missing in the Napoleonic epic, but it is not too early for a summing up. French schoolbooks teach that Napoleon's glory cost France the loss of her natural frontiers, vast sums of money, an appalling number of lives. True. From a French point of view the Napoleonic age was indeed a costly one. But his role transcends mere national boundaries. Napoleon, and the Revolution of which he was the product, cannot be considered from an exclusively French point of view. From a European standpoint, the benefits he bestowed upon the then "emerging nations" were incalculable, albeit often involuntary.

His passion for centralizing and unifying gave an impetus to the reshaping of old Europe that continued even after his downfall. Although he had tried to suppress in France many of the principles set forth by the French Revolution, he spread those principles elsewhere in Europe, notably in Spain, Germany and Italy. His last wish would have been to promote a united Germany, yet his reduction of the number of fragmentary German principalities was to do just that. Nor did he have any desire to unite Italy; yet by giving the Italians a taste of national independence he set their unification in motion. His brutal and senseless oppression of the Spaniards aroused in them a burning nationalism.

By his victories and conquests he demonstrated the rottenness of the old order and the need for reform, and his unfulfilled promises to "liberated" lands gave them a taste of freedom which spurred them to greater nationalistic and united efforts. His very insensibility and the oppressive measures he took against them spurred them to action and gave them a sense of dignity and importance that no mere decree could have done. His shabby treatment of the Pope gave the Church a moral authority such as it had not had for centuries. His greatest wish had been to strengthen his own imperial power, yet by treating kings as though they were clerks, by showing up the moral decay of European sovereigns, he dealt the final blow to European monarchy.

When he began his career he found the old world in chaos. He was certainly an opportunist who picked up the pieces and put them together to his own and his family's advantage, but he also preserved some of the reforms and innovations that the new order had imposed. During the four years of relative peace that lasted from 1809 to 1812 he laid down the bare foundation of the precursor to the European Common Market—the Continental Block against England. The Napoleonic Code has already been mentioned elsewhere. He wanted peace, but he never learned that it could not be won through wars. His own aversion to ideologies and the excesses to which they so often give rise made him forget the value of moral forces.

Perhaps his greatest contribution—and it is of doubtful merit—is the revolution he brought about in the techniques of power and the manipulation of men. The "image" he projected was an inspiring and impressive one, compounded of grandeur (the Emperor), humility (the "Little Corporal") and glory (the victor of countless battles). And he used every available means of propaganda: the press, the war bulletins, the pageantry of a noble Empire, the artful creation of his own legend.

At St. Helena, where he had the bitter privilege of becoming his own historian, Napoleon boasted not of his military conquests, but of his administrative reforms. He was an ambivalent man, typical of an era of transition, who represented the 18th century, the age of Enlightenment and of the Revolution, and the 19th century, the age of Nationalism and the Rights of Man. Napoleon's stature was too great for France, too small for Europe.

THE LIGHTNING RETURN FROM ELBA

Napoleon's journey to Elba became increasingly difficult as he approached the south of France where, since the month of March, monarchist agents had been active. They had even consigned Bordeaux to the English on March 12. The Count of Provence, the future King Louis XVIII, had urged the French, in a widely circulated proclamation, to welcome as friends the "generous allies," to open the gates of their cities, to avoid a "criminal and futile resistance" and to welcome their entry into France with "cries of joy." After Avignon, on its way through the small town Orgon, the Emperor's carriage was surrounded by hostile demonstrators.

On February 26, 1815, after 10 months on Elba, Napoleon left the island, landed on March 1 near Antibes, and with a handful of men, about 700 of them, made the trip in 20 days from the French Mediterranean to the Palace of the Tuileries in Paris. This was the beginning of the last act of the play, or rather the epilogue of his tragedy. It became known as the "Hundred Days."

Why the return? And why were the very ones who had boasted of having put him behind bars, as if he had been a dangerous beast, the first to receive him with open arms? It had taken only a few months for the Bourbons to do everything possible to make the people long for the return of Napoleon. In their wake had come the *émigrés*, thirsty for impossible revenge. From then on it was generally accepted that they had learned nothing, forgotten nothing—in short, they had understood nothing of what had happened. For them the "restoration," that vague term, meant but one thing: the abolition of everything that the Revolution had brought about, the wiping out of its benefits as well as those conferred by the Empire, the reestablishment, exactly as it had been, of the Old Regime. This was patently unfeasible, national sentiment had altered too much for such a retrogression.

This time Napoleon was returning to save revolutionary France from the reactionaries and presented himself in a liberal guise that scarcely suited him. He had the whole-hearted support of the army, and he could easily believe that the entire nation stood behind him. Lazare Carnot, the former deputy to the Convention who in the days of the Republic had been called, and rightly so, the organizer of victory and who had had the courage in 1804 to vote against the Empire, flew to his side. He had Benjamin Constant, a liberal writer who had been, in happier times, one of his bitterest critics, draw up a new constitution, but the customary plebiscite brought out a very small vote: Out of 6,000,000 voters, only 1,310,000 went to the polls. The enthusiasm which had greeted Napoleon's return turned out to be little more than a spark. His return came to seem as impossible as the Bourbons', for it too was a turning back.

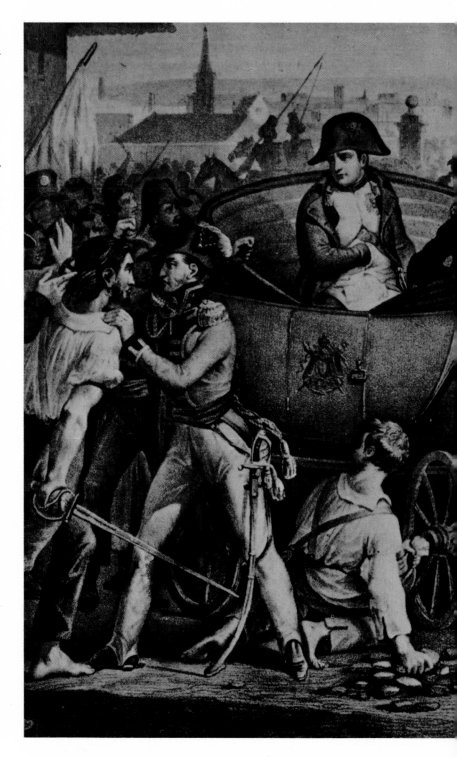

Bonaparte's return to Paris took place on the morning of March 20, 1815. The print below depicts his festive, triumphal reception at the Tuileries Palace. The cheering crowd was probably the same one that had the day before, saluted Louis XVIII, who had by this time discreetly retired from the scene. Russia and Austria had hesitated before restoring the Bourbons to the throne; the Csar had at first been decidedly against it. Only the English, who had granted asylum to Louis XVIII from 1807 on and who had made him an annual allowance, were steadfastly in favor of his restoration. The king's sojourn in the Tuileries had lasted little more than 10 months. Barely 24 hours elapsed between his departure and Napoleon's arrival.

A miniature of Maria Walenska which was found in Genappe in the carriage abandoned by Napoleon after Waterloo. This is one of the rare portraits of the Polish countess, perhaps the only woman in Napoleon's life whose romantic interest in him was entirely disinterested. The Emperor had met her in Warsaw in the interval between the battles of Jena, October 13, 1806, and of Eylau, February 8, 1807. She was 22 years old and married to an old bore. (Napoleon was 37, accustomed by now to having Europe at his feet.) The short romance, which came to an end with his departure, produced a son. She retired into obscurity, reappearing only discreetly, to join him on Elba. (There was also another lady on Elba, Napoleon's mother.)

WATERLOO:
THE DESPERATE BATTLE

Napoleon at Waterloo is the caption for the lithograph, a portion of which is reproduced above. He is seen surrounded by his generals, who are described as "putting their hands to the sword and becoming soldiers once more." The old Grenadiers, fearful for the Emperor's safety, implore him to retire. Note, in the lower right corner, Bertrand's hand on the bridle of the Emperor's horse whom he was hoping to lead away from the melee. Count

Bertrand had been the grand marshal of the palace and followed him later into exile on St. Helena. Opposite: The unsuccessful attempt by the French to capture the factory of La Haye-Sainte on June 18, 1815, in a contemporary print now at the British Museum. The English infantry put up a memorable resistance. Overleaf: Sir William Allan's painting, at the Wellington Museum, of the Battle of Waterloo.

The battle of Waterloo might well have been called the battle of the Belle Alliance, the name of the place, 12 miles south of Brussels on the road to Genappe, where the two victorious allied leaders, the 46-year-old English Duke of Wellington and the 73-year-old Prussian General Blücher, met late on Sunday June 18, 1815 after the last of Napoleon's forces had been beaten. The name of this small hamlet was symbolic, for the alliance finally had triumphed, but at the cost of 45,000 men dead or dying. The battle took place in an area of roughly three square miles. Wellington's Anglo-Dutch forces were deployed in a solid line south of Mont-Saint-Jean to cut off the road to Brussels. Two days before Napoleon had beaten Blücher at Ligny and having ordered General Grouchy to pursue the Prussians he had turned to face the English himself.

There are so many famous descriptions of the battle of Waterloo that it seems superfluous to record here the ups and downs of the battle. A violent rain storm on the preceding day had forced Napoleon to delay the action until nearly midday. The first attack of the French infantry against Wellington having failed—the latter really had earned his nickname of the "Iron Duke"—Napoleon threw Ney's cavalry, 10,000 strong, a veritable "sea of steel," to the assault of Mont-Saint-Jean. But after three hours of struggle without having dented English resistance, Ney had to abandon the height. Toward 7:30 P.M., after the Prussians had been thrown back, Napoleon tried one final attack with his grenadiers, but English fire, rapid and precise, mowed down two thirds of his battalions. At this crucial moment the long-awaited Blücher arrived with his reinforcements in the rumble of thunder made by his Prussians. Grouchy failed altogether to put in an appearance. It was the end. The French were routed. Only the remains of the Old Guard fought on doggedly to protect Napoleon's retreat.

And so at Waterloo Napoleon's bold plan to regain his empire failed. Pulled along by the remnants of his defeated army he found himself once more in Paris where toward the end of June 1815 he abdicated one last time.

EXILE TO ST. HELENA

Below, a contemporary print showing the historic meeting between Blücher and Wellington after Waterloo. The aged Blücher embraces Wellington, calling him "mein lieber Kamerad"—"my dear friend." Bottom of the page, an aquarelle by G. Opiz, showing one aspect of the occupation of Paris by the Allies:

a bivouac of Cossacks on the Champs Elysées. The King of Prussia, the Csar and the Prince of Schwarzenberg had entered the city at the head of their troops on April 1, 1814. The monarchs, overjoyed by Napoleon's fall and the return of Louis XVIII to the French throne, tried to pull down the statue at the top of the Colonne Vendôme.

On July 3, 1815, on the very day when Paris capitulated once more, Napoleon had reached Rochefort, at the mouth of the Charente. It is a small town with a population of 30,000 which takes pride in being the birthplace of a writer of sea stories, Pierre Loti. In those days, Rochefort-sur-Mer (on the sea) was an important port. For this reason it was under British blockade.

Napoleon, who had been planning to sail for the United States, gave up that nebulous plan and instead entrusted himself to the British Government, asking them, in modern terms, for political asylum. "Your Royal Highness," he wrote to the Prince Regent: "The victim of the factions that divide my country and of the hostility of the great European powers, I have ended my political career and I come, as Themistocles did, to claim a seat by the hearth of the British people. I put myself under the protection of British law, which I claim from your Royal Highness as the most powerful, most constant, and most generous of my enemies." But already since the month of March he had been banned from Europe by the Allied powers, who were meeting at the Congress of Vienna. The delegates of the rulers had finally accomplished what the Council of Five Hundred had failed to do during the tempestuous meeting of the 19 Brumaire: They had abandoned Napoleon to "public revenge," as it was described. The former Emperor had become a war criminal. If he wasn't labeled such at the time, it was only because the term had not yet come into use. Instead he was considered a prisoner of war from the time, on July 18 when he boarded *H.M.S. Bellerophon* in the port of Rochefort and throughout his various transfers, until he reached the island of St. Helena, at the end of nowhere, off the West African coast. The long trip from Plymouth, England, on board the *Northumberland* lasted 70 days.

One month before his departure, in the evening of July 8, Louis XVIII had returned to the Tuileries Palace. In his welcoming speech, at the gates of Paris, the prefect Chabrol noted that "one hundred days" had passed since the beloved king, amid the tears of his people, had been obliged to flee. That small, insignificant, obsequious official could never have guessed that he had contributed so dramatic a description to the last Napoleonic flare.

*Left, Napoleon's embarkation
on the British ship Bellerophon
in the port of Rochefort,
as drawn by Beaujet.
The troops lined up on the
bridge did not present arms.
Captain Maitland was the skipper.
The ship sailed straight
to Plymouth. From here,
on August 8, 1815, Napoleon
left for St. Helena.*

*The print above shows
Napoleon, during his imprisonment,
trying to keep death at a
distance. Lt. Gen. Sir Hudson
Lowe had been made governor
of St. Helena to keep
an eye on "the prisoner of
war." The Bonapartists
saw in him "an
extraordinary animal"
(See print below.)*

71

Below, Napoleon's deathbed scene according to a contemporary print. The dying man is surrounded by some of his companions in exile: Count Henri Bertrand with his wife and child at the foot of the bed; Gen. Charles Tristan Montholon, seated in the chair by the head of the bed; two Englishmen, a doctor and a captain. During his final illness his attending physician was a Corsican, Doctor Antommarchi, who had been sent to St. Helena by the aging "Madame Mère" who survived her son. She spent the remainder of her life in Rome. The cause of Napoleon's death, a recently reopened discussion, has been sometimes ascribed to poisoning.

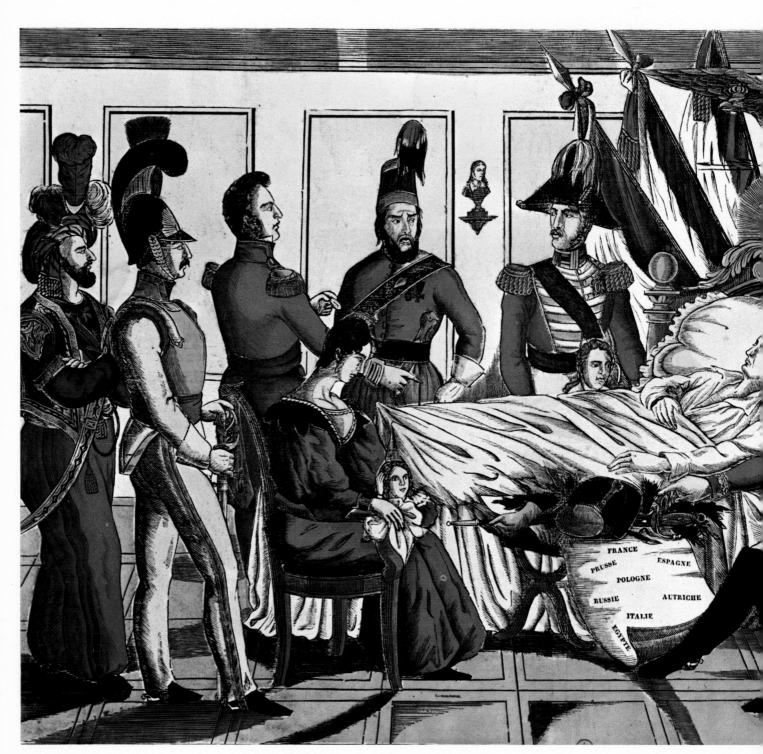

AFTER DEATH: AGAIN THE GREAT EMPEROR

During the second half of the last century, the French Third Republic was temporarily and unexpectedly caught up in a wave of popularity for a certain General Boulanger, who later committed suicide. He seemed to be the hero of another outburst of "Bonapartism"—*i.e.*, a species of politico-military dictatorship. From the back benches of the government a dissident shouted at him, "At your age Napoleon was already dead!" The sentence does not make much sense, but it made a deep impression on the public. The point of the episode, which is basically insignificant, is to highlight how strong was the myth of Napoleon's uniqueness and personal mystique even long after his death.

He died at five in the afternoon of May 5, 1821, before his 52nd birthday, after six years of prison. Volumes have been written on the subject of that imprisonment; much has been said on the treatment he received at the hands of his jailers on the island ten miles long by six miles wide, 1,200 miles from Africa, more than 1,800 miles from America. Today we must admit that no better fate could have befallen the former Emperor. At least, in view of more recent times, he certainly fared better than he might have. Even then "Perfidious Albion" proved herself wiser than those who were loudly asking for the summary execution of the "outlaw" or the condemnation pronounced by a tribunal made up of representatives of the rulers of Europe. And furthermore it was England herself which 20 years later took the initiative in having Napoleon's ashes restored to France. The painful years of the "atonement," coming after 20 years of the most glorious splendor, had conferred upon him the halo of martyrdom. The Napoleonic legend was already in being, constantly being added to by poets and artists. Napoleon had become an epic hero. One of the greatest French romantic poets and novelists, Victor Hugo, had become the chief glorifier of his deeds.

It fell to the lot of the most bourgeois king France was ever to know—Louis Philippe of Bourbon-Orléans, who reigned from 1830 to 1848, the son of Philippe Egalité, popularly known as the "umbrella king" because he always carried one—to preside over the solemn reinterment of Napoleon's ashes under the dome of the Invalides (another of the Napoleonic monuments) on December 15, 1840. Henceforth only his glory survived.

Above, a lithograph of Monthelier showing the ashes of Napoleon leaving the land of his exile on October 16, 1840. On December 15 of the same year, after a journey across France, the solemn reinterment of his ashes took place at the Invalides in Paris. Below, a snuffbox showing the tombstone in St. Helena with, between the willows, the full-length profile of Napoleon.

The Awakening is the title
of one of the most famous
lithographs done by Raffet on
the Napoleonic epic. To the
rolling of drums beating a
charge the dead reawaken,
grope for their arms,
try to get on their feet
and form into line,
ready once more to shout
"Vive l'Empereur."
There is a breath of epic
glory in this realistic
print. Sentimental though it
may be, it is symbolic of
the Napoleonic legend which
came to full bloom during
his 20-year career and soared
to the heights of poetry after
the death of the Emperor.

"He is Robespierre on horseback." This concise and somewhat malicious description of Napoleon by one of his most persistent foes, the writer Madame de Staël, is still valid, a century and a half later. Just as the Reign of Terror was a natural result of the Revolution, so the Empire sprang naturally from its dictatorship. And like Madame de Staël's metaphor, the Empire also galloped beyond the frontiers of France. Those extremists, the Jacobins, had at one point made an appeal to an internationalism of common people rather than to an internationalism of princes. They had pitted themselves and their revolutionary principles against the despots who had formed a coalition for a "holy war" against Revolutionary France. Napoleon changed the perspectives. The men of the Revolution looked to the frontiers of the Rhine; he looked to Italy; they had thought of France in terms of Europe; he went to Egypt and distant Russia to seek the Near East. The Empire made of a national revolution a European fact. The Napoleonic Empire which was the product of the French Revolution left an indelible print on Europe.

1769 — August 15: his birth in Ajaccio.

1779-1785 — Cadet at the military schools of Brienne and Paris. Made 2nd lieutenant on October 28, 1785.

1792 — October 15: return to Corsica. Made lieutenant colonel in the National Guard. Break with Pasquale Paoli.

1793 — February: expedition to La Maddalena (Sardinia). June: sails for France with his family. December: siege of Toulon. Made brigadier general.

1795 — October 26: commander of the army of the Interior.

1796 — March 9: marriage with Joséphine de Beauharnais. Commander-in-Chief of the Army of Italy. March-April: beginning of the Italian campaign. Defeats the Austrians at Montenotte and Dego, the Piedmontese at Millesimo and Mondovi. April 28: The Armistice of Cherasco between the Kingdom of Sardinia and France. May 10, August 3-4, November 15-17: defeats the Austrians at Lodi, Lonato, Castiglione and Arcole.

1797 — January 14: battle of Rivoli. February 2: fall of Mantua. April 18: preliminary peace negotiations with Austria at Leoben. October 17: Treaty of Campoformio.

1798 — May 19: embarkation from Toulon, beginning of the Egyptian campaign. June 30: landing at Aboukir and conquest of Alexandria. August 1: Nelson destroys the French fleet at the Battle of the Nile.

1799 — February: Syrian campaign. August 22: embarkation for France. October 9: landing at Fréjus. November 9: transfer of the Council of Five Hundred to Saint-Cloud. November 10: setting up the Consulate and appointment of the First Consul.

1800 — May-June: second Italian campaign. May 15-20: crossing of the Alps. June 14: battle of Marengo, defeat of the Austrians. December 24: assassination plot in Paris.

1801 — February 9: Peace Treaty of Lunéville with the Austrians. August 15: signing of the Concordat between Church and state.

1802 — March 25: Peace of Amiens with England. August 4: named Consul for life.

1803 — May 17: violation of the Treaty of Amiens by England.

1804 — March 20: shooting of the Duc d'Enghien. May 18: proclamation of the Empire. December 2: Coronation at Notre Dame.

1805 — April-August: third coalition (England, Russia, Germany, Sweden and Naples). October 14 and 20: battle of Elchingen against Austria and fall of Ulm. October 21: the English defeat the French fleet at Trafalgar. December 2: battle of Austerlitz and defeat of the Russians and Austrians. December 26: Treaty of Pressburg with Austria.

1806 — Fourth coalition (Prussia, Russia, England). October: Saxon campaign against Prussia. October 13: defeat of the Prussians at Jena and Auerstädt. October 27: entrance into Berlin and proclamation of the Continental Blockade against England.

1807 — February 8: battle of Eylau, against Russia. June 14: defeat of the Russians at Friedland. July 8: Tilsit Treaty of Peace and Alliance between Russia and France.

1808 — March 23, intervention in Spain. May 2: insurrection of Madrid and French reprisals. July 22: Surrender of the French troops at Bailén.

1809 — March: fifth coalition (Austria, England, Spain). April 19-23: Bavarian campaign, surrender of Ratisbon. May 21-22: French defeat at Aspern. July 5-6: Napoleon crosses the Danube and defeats the Austrians at Wagram. October 14: peace treaty at Vienna between Austria and France. December 15: divorce from Joséphine.

1810 — April 1: marriage with Marie Louise of Austria.

1811 — March 20: birth of the King of Rome.

1812 — Sixth coalition (England, Russia, Sweden). Russian campaign. June 24-26: the French army crosses the Niemen. September 7: Russian defeat at Borodino. September 13: occupation of Moscow. October 24: beginning of the retreat. November 25-29: crossing of the Berezina. December 5: the Emperor's return to Paris.

1813 — German campaign. May 1-2 and 19: the French defeat the Allies at Lützen and Bautzen. June 4: Armistice of Plasvitz. June 27: General Coalition (England, Austria, Russia, Prussia). October 16-19: the Allies defeat France at Leipzig. December 21: the Allied armies cross the Rhine.

1814 — February: the French try to stop the Allies in numerous battles. March 30: battle and fall of Paris. April 6: abdication at Fontainebleau. April 20: departure for Elba. May 30: first Treaty of Paris between the Allies and France.

1815 — February 26: Napoleon leaves Elba. March 1: landing at Golfe Juan. March 20: return to Paris. June: Belgian campaign and Prussian defeat at Ligny. June 18: defeat at Waterloo. June 22: second abdication. July 3: fall of Paris. July 18: embarkation for exile. November 20: second Treaty of Paris.

1821 — May 5: death on St. Helena.